Spiritual Combat

By Simene' Walden

SPIRITUAL COMBAT by SIMENE' WALDEN

Published by THE STUDENT TEACHER
P.O. BOX 813
SAVAGE, MD 20763
www.simenwalden.com

© 2017 Simene' Walden

All rights reserved. No part of this publication may be reproduced, stored in a retrieval system, or transmitted, in any form or in any means – by electronic, mechanical, photocopying, recording or otherwise – without prior written permission, except as permitted by U.S. copyright law.

ISBN: 978-0-999797-2-0

Thank you for respecting the proprietary work of the author.

Cover Design: JAMIL ABBAS

Editor: ADENIKE WILHEIMS

All scripture quotations, unless otherwise noted, are taken from the King James Bible.

Scripture quotations, noted *NKJV*, are taken from the New King James Bible. Copyright ©1979, 1980, 1982, 1984 by Thomas Nelson, Inc. Used by permission. All rights reserved.

Scripture quotations, noted *NLT* are taken from the New Living Translation Bible. Copyright © 1996 Tyndale House. Used by permission. All rights reserved.

Scripture quotations, noted *The Message* are taken from The Message Bible: The Bible in Contemporary English. Copyright © 1993, 1994, 1995, 1996, 2000, and 2001, 2002. NavPress Publishing Group. Used by permission. All rights reserved.

Scripture quotations, noted *NIV* are taken from The Holy Bible: The New International Version. Copyright © 1973, 1978, and 1984. International Bible Society. Used by permission of Zonderan. All rights reserved.

First Printing, August 2017

Printed in the United States of America

Contents

About the Author vii

Testimonials from *Standing On His Words* xi

Standing On His Words Courses and Seminars xiii

Dedication xviii

Why Should We Pray? 1

What is Combat? 3

Battle Ready Prayer 7

Combat Declarations and Affirmations 11

Spiritual Combat Prayers 13

    Cup of Wine Prayer 13

    Sinful Nature Prayer 15

    Torrential Rain of Fire Prayer 19

    Release From Demonic Dreams Prayer 21

    Healing Prayer 27

    Rivers of Blood Prayer 29

    Wind of God Prayer 31

    The Breaker's Prayer 37

    Dispatchers Prayer 41

    Fallen Enemy Prayer 43

    satan Clause Prayer 45

    An APB Prayer 47

    Back Slider Prayer 51

Benediction 57

About the Author

Simene' Walden also known as "The Student Teacher" was given that name by the Holy Ghost on June 7, 2016 during an early morning chat session. Simene' is a teacher by vocation but is a student first. Simene' is an accountability coach, speaker, teacher, writer, and 3X best selling author on amazon. She is the Chief Operating Officer of her business called *The Student Teacher*.

She is a life-long learner; always looking to grow spiritually, physically, mentally, emotionally, and psychologically by seeking out new, revelatory, and relevant information. She has thirteen years of public school teaching experience and her greatest teachers, aside from God, have been the students she serves. Simene' s desire is to have a positive and Christ-like influence on this now and next generation.

Simene' is a native of North Carolina, but resides in Laurel, MD. In 2004, Walden graduated from Fayetteville State University with a Bachelors of Arts Degree in English & Literature. In 2014, she graduated from Grand Canyon University with a Master's of Arts Degree in Christian Studies with an Emphasis on Youth Ministry.

Simené's primary objective is to teach others everything she has learned so they, too, can be empowered, educated, and equipped. She is active in her local church, Temple of Praise International Church, in Beltsville, Maryland, where she serves in various ministries. Simene' received a prayer mantle from her Apostle Nike Wilheims on November 27, 2016. Her apostle prayed that a spirit of prayer would come upon her. She prayed that Simene' would be a fisher of men and the mantle of Daniel, Jehu, and a double mantle of prayed that was upon her life, be poured upon Simene'. Simene's life was forever changed.

You can find God's servant sharing her love for God on her social media sites as well on the streets of Washington, DC. She has recently launched her business *The Student Teacher* where she is flooding the Educational System with God's Words of prayer.

Contact the author:

thestudentteacher17@gmail.com

http://www.simenewalden.com

https://www.facebook.com/thestudenteacher

http://www.twitter.com/@simenewalden

http://periscope.tv/@simenewalden

http://instagram.com/simenewalden

Mailing Address: P.O. Box 813 Savage, MD 20763

If you are interested in special quantity discounts for bulk purchases please contact the author directly via email @thestudentteacher17@gmail.com.

On Another Note (OAN): Consider leaving a review on Amazon. Now suit up so you can go to war. FOCUS on PRAYER!

Freedom

Over

Cluttered

Unwanted

Situations

On

Putting

Request

At

Yeshua's

Ear

Regularly

Testimonials from "Standing On His Words: Prayers and Devotionals Every Educator Can Pray"

Recently, I purchased, Standing on His Words, by Simene' Walden because I was interested in learning about how I could spiritually address many of the challenges within the educational system. From the first prayer, Empowering Educators Through Prayer, I was captivated by the power and passion that was outlined as she exposes the devil in schools across the world! Each prayer addresses the reasons why prayer is important for all of us regardless of whether we are educators, administrators, or parents. As an administrator, there is a prayer that directly speaks to preparing my heart to address the needs of my schools in a professional Christ-like way as opposed to the way of the world. My favorite is chapter called, Prayers for Intercessors Praying for the Educational System. This chapter is call to action for all people to confront the specific challenges close to their hearts and intercede through prayer. As a mother, I have prayed several devotions from this book over my child daily, and I am looking forward to using it in conjunction with my Bible as there is specific scripture that that accompanies each devotion. I cannot wait to see the manifestation of God's power through these prayers! Thank you, Simene' for writing this book to encourage us as adults to pray for our children and ourselves to be better stewards over the God's Kingdom. I stand with you in the movement of #praying4schools through #StandingonHisWords.

(Alma, Amazon Review)

Both as an advocate for Moms in Prayer, an Educator and a mom myself, I find this resource to be invaluable! The power of prayer is monumental and we need it now more than ever! Excellent guide!

(Anita, Amazon Review)

As an educator, I recommend this book to my fellow educator as a reminder of why we do what we do. Get your copy today!

(Aikyna, Amazon Review)

This book is one to not only Read BUT keep out ON your desk !! Soooo many great insights and prayers for sooo many at different stages AND struggles as well!! GREAT reference !!! A Definite book to get for all!!!!!

(Kelly, Amazon Review)

It is good you are sharing your gift with the world, and educators in particular. I haven't read a book on this topic yet. Thanks again.

(Deborah, Colleague)

Standing On His Words Courses and Seminars

Young Adults (17-24)

The Struggle Is Real: Parents Just Don't Understand

Do you often bump heads with your teenager and/or young adult? Do they feel like they are always being corrected for doing something wrong that they actually believe is right? Do they seem lost and frustrated because they want to create the life God has for them, but they have no idea what that is and what that looks like? If you answered yes to either of these questions, this seminar is for your child!

This seminar will give your child real-solutions to very real problems in a very real and aggressive world. Within this workshop, teenagers and young adults will learn how to perfect the areas of concern in their lives from biblical truths and practical teaching.

The four modules will include the following:

1. How to create a blueprint for your life?
2. How to take the opinions of others and learn from them?
3. How to talk to God and get real-time answers?
4. How to focus on yourself and become the Best YOU?

Adults (25-40)

The Struggle Is Real: People Just Don't Understand

Do you often bump heads with people? Are you criticized about the way you see things and how you live your life? Do you often feel like the people around you do not relate to you and don't understand your viewpoint on many things?

This seminar will give you real-solutions to your very real problems in a very real and aggressive world. In this class, you will learn how to perfect the areas of concern in your life from biblical truths and practical teaching.

The four modules will include the following:

1. How to create a blueprint for your life?
2. How to take the opinions of others and learn from them?
3. How to talk to God and get real-time answers?
4. How to focus on yourself and become the Best YOU?

(Educators, Leaders, Administrators)

Creating a Culture of Collaboration and Respect

As the demands of excellence, production, and results are eminent, do you desire to respect all children regardless of their behaviors and interactions with you? Do you wish to respect and gain respect from fellow colleagues? Do you work in an atmosphere that could use some positive TLC?

In this class, you will learn how to create a place of peace in the environments that seem to be dominated by drama, negativity, and hostility.

The six modules will include the following:

1. How to create a culturally sensitive and affirmative environment?
2. How to create an Educational Environment not mirrored by the image of the Penal System?
3. How to protect yourself from being influenced by the accusations of others?
4. How to minimize distractions in the workforce?
5. How to honestly communicate with others even when angry?

Additional Seminars and Courses Include:

How to avoid "burn out"?

How to have the heart of a teacher and not just the knowledge of one?

Each seminar and course is a 4-hour session that includes the book and all other materials.

Additional Books By The Author:

Standing On His Words: Prayers and Devotionals Every Educator Can Pray (Print Book) @**bit.ly/2StandBook**

Standing On His Words: Prayers and Devotionals Every Educator Can Pray Ebook @ **bit.ly/2Stand**

Standing On His Words: Prayers and Devotionals Every Educator Can Pray Workbook @ **bit.ly/2StandingWB**

Spiritual Combat EBook @**bit.ly/combatprayer**

My Heart Under A Microscope Print Book
@**bit.ly/heartunderscope**

The Student Teacher Quotes Print Book
@**bit.ly/studentteacherquotes**

Coming 2018

Standing On His Words: Student Edition

#youthNcrisis

Free Yourself

A Daughter's Cry To Her Fathers

A Family on The Altar Alters a Family

For booking inquiries and speaking engagements, please contact the author directly via email @thestudentteacher17@gmail.com.

Dedication

Father, you are my Lord and Savior. I dedicate this book to you as you own my life and you have yet spared me again. I give these prayers back to you out of a place of surrender, sacrifice, and gratitude. Thank you for saving my natural life yet again. You spoke to me and told me what could have happened but it was not in your divine timing that I should be taken from this earth as of now. As I record what you spoke to me, may every reader self examine their lives to make sure they are in right standing with you; for we know not the day or hour in which you shall return or we shall meet you.

The Lord showed me that at 3:11 PM on July 22, 2017 outside of Warrenton, VA, had I not been in his timing. I would have died in a car accident after a pick up truck ran into the passenger side where I was sitting when my friend pulled out into the wrong lane of traffic. Officer Tommy or Timothy Jackson was going to be the officer that arrived on the scene first to pronounce me dead.

It would have been a case where my mom would have said, "I just got off the phone with her". We talked at 2:21 PM about my book signing in September. She asked what I was doing and I said, "Riding in the car". The last thing she said was, "Ok, go ahead and finish riding in the car". She had no idea and neither did I, that that could have been my last ride twenty minutes later. But God is faithful. The good work he has started in me, he will perfect.

Lord, I give you my life again today. I give you another yes for today and I completely surrender my will to yours in Jesus Name.

Why Should We Pray?

We should pray because God commands us to pray. God has assured us that when we pray anything in His name that is aligned with His Word and will for our lives, He will answer it. God will never answer a wish but he will answer His Word. God will never answer our emotions because unlike Him, our emotions change. God can and will answer a prayer prayed in faith that will sustain our emotions. It is God's Word that is constant. The Word of God and God are inseparable. Those two are the same yesterday, today, and forever more.

Is anyone among you suffering? Let him pray. Is anyone cheerful? Let him sing psalms. Is anyone among you sick? Let him call for the elders of the church, and let them pray over him, anointing him with oil in the name of the Lord. And the prayer of faith will save the sick, and the Lord will raise him up. And if he has committed sins, he will be forgiven. Confess *your* trespasses to one another, and pray for one another, that you may be healed. The effective, fervent prayer of a righteous man avails much. Elijah was a man with a nature like ours, and he prayed earnestly that it would not rain; and it did not rain on the land for three years and six months. And he prayed again, and the heaven gave rain, and the earth produced its fruit. **(James 5: 13-18)**

Continue earnestly in prayer, being vigilant in it with thanksgiving. **(Colossians 4: 2)**

For the eyes of the Lord *are* on the righteous, And His ears *are open* to their prayers; But the face of the Lord *is* against those who do evil." **(1 Peter 3: 12)**

Be anxious for nothing, but in everything by prayer and supplication, with thanksgiving, let your requests be made known to God; **7** and the peace of God, which surpasses all understanding, will guard your hearts and minds through Christ Jesus. **(Philippians 4: 6-7)**

What is Combat?

Combat can be defined as a fight or contest between individuals or groups. It can also be defined as conflict, controversy, or active fighting in a war. We are not fighting against people with bodies that we can see, but we are fighting against spirits without bodies that we cannot see. Instead of tearing one another down, we must engage the enemy, fight, and win in prayer. Put on your whole armor of God, strap up your boots and let's war in the spirit. **(2 Corinthians 6: 7)**

Then David said to the Philistine, "You come to me with a sword, with a spear, and with a javelin. But I come to you in the name of the Lord of hosts, the God of the armies of Israel, whom you have defied. **(1 Samuel 17:45)**

Finally, my brethren, be strong in the Lord and in the power of His might. Put on the whole armor of God, that you may be able to stand against the wiles of the devil. For we do not wrestle against flesh and blood, but against principalities, against powers, against the rulers of the darkness of this age, against spiritual *hosts* of wickedness in the heavenly *places*. Therefore take up the whole armor of God, that you may be able to withstand in the evil day, and having done all, to stand. Stand therefore, having girded your waist with truth, having put on the breastplate of righteousness, and having shod your feet with the preparation of the gospel of peace; above all, taking the shield of faith with which you will be able to quench all the fiery darts of the wicked one. And take the helmet of salvation, and the sword of the Spirit, which is the word of God; praying always with all prayer and supplication in the Spirit, being watchful to this end with all perseverance and supplication for all the saints **(Ephesians 6: 10-18)**

This passage of Scripture provides believers with the suitable equipment and the guiding principles on how to operate and defeat the enemy. When planning for combat, the belt would have been the primary piece of defensive gear put on by a Roman soldier. The belt trains one to be ready for battle. As a Christian, you need to be ready to protect yourself against the powers of darkness and not be oblivious and ignorant. As a leader, one must be prepared in all situations. When it comes to the breastplate, the Roman soldier would have fastened it around the chest to protect vital organs. Righteousness must be worn as a breastplate in order to war against inequality and dishonesty. Righteousness helps reinstate harmony and order in our homes, in our businesses, in our ministries, in the land, and any other situation we may face. God extends his righteousness to every believer in Jesus Christ and it is not anything we can achieve by doing good deeds.

However, we must have the mind of Christ to perform actions and good deeds as Christ did. Marching was an indispensable part of a soldier's life, and no soldier could rally without well-built, strong shoes. Breaking of a soldier's shoes was a metaphor for flaws or trounce. The studded shoes permitted the soldier to stand firm. Without the shoes, the soldier could not retain his position against the enemy. The gospel of peace is when we have tranquility with God. When situations arise, we must seek God first to give us answers and then a peace about them. The shield was made from goatskin or calfskin that was laid over sturdy pieces of wood. Before going into battle, the soldier was drenched in water so when the flames from the fiery arrow was thrown, the water would immediately extinguish them. The shield of faith is a believer's protection against temptation. When tempted in any situation, one must remember that the faith you have in God can get you through any situation. Any distraction that the enemy brings can be counterattacked by one's faith in God. As far as the helmet is concerned, it was formed from bronze in iron and the two-hinged cheek, sections the sides of a soldier's face. The helmet protected the skull and neck from the enemy. The helmet points to God's final victory on the cross and over all forces of the enemy. Salvation for a believer can ensure that all sin can be forgiven. Salvation for a believer ensures that Jesus has already defeated all evil in this world. As a believer, we must walk in the assurance of the finished work and continue to strive for excellence in our daily walk with God.

Unlike all the other armor, the sword was used to back down the enemy and not necessarily to protect us from the enemy. The sword, which is the bible, was usually crafted from iron and there was an extra coating on the blade. The Word is a believer's offensive weapon to defeat the enemy. When someone is being attacked, one must ensure that they have the Word on the inside and readily available for use. If you ever find yourself in an unusual or uncomfortable situation, the Word will back down the plans of the enemy, silence them, and provide you with instructions on how to react.

The helmet, shield, breastplate, belt, sword, and gospel all provide you with the necessary tools to overcome sin. As we rely on God and study his Word, we will know how to act, what is appropriate and not appropriate according to the Bible, and how to respond God's way to others. I think the greatest cause of poor ethical decisions is not studying the bible and seeing what God says about the matter. There are instructions for every area of your life in the bible, but when you start to rely on flesh, emotions, and the world, judgments become tainted, evil, and sinful. When you are not studying and you have no spiritual guide to show you your faults, you make unfortunate decisions. Study to show yourself approved. Hide God's word in your heart so you will not sin against Him. Repent if needed and get ready for battle.

Battle Ready Prayer

Father God, I thank You for being God and God all by yourself. Thank you Father that you are King of Kings and Lord of Lords. Father, I believe that Jesus is the worthy Lamb that was slaughtered to receive power, riches, wisdom, strength, honor, glory, and blessings. Father I exchange my thoughts for your thoughts today and declare that I have the mind of Christ. I confess with my mouth and believe in my heart that you are the way, truth, and the life. I receive You in my heart today as Your child. I accept You as my Lord and Savior. Blot out my sins today and wash me from all of my issues, problems, sins, and iniquities. I acknowledge that I have sinned against You. I was shapen in iniquity from a child, but You desire me to be truthful and honest. I commit to being truthful and honest from this day forward. Come into my heart and change me for your glory. Even when I walk through the darkest valley, I know You are there to protect and comfort me. Thank you preparing a table before my enemies. Surely your goodness and mercy shall follow me all the days of my life. I know that you give the angels charge over me according to Psalms 91. Thank you for divine protection. God you are my fortress and refuge. I trust in you. Thank you delivering me from every snare that wanted to and still wants to entrap me. I declare and decree that you are my buckler and my shield. Thank you for your protection over and over again. Thank you for your protection when I willfully put myself in harm's way. Thank you for your protection when others put me in harm's way. Thank you for your protection when the enemy set me up for my demise, but the blood of Jesus spoke and still speaks better things than the blood of Abel. I apply that same blood over my doorpost now. Wherever I call home, I apply the blood of Jesus over it right now and the death angel and any plagues that has been assigned to me, has just now been destroyed by the fire and power of the Lord Jesus Christ. I crush the head of the serpent now and I walk in the power and authority you have given me in Jesus Name.

Father according to Ephesians 6: 13- 18, I put on the whole armour of God today and I keep it on. I put on the belt of truth. My shoes are full of peace that passes all understanding. My peace is the peace that you give Oh Mighty God. I have on the shield of faith. My faith is in you and it's my hope of things that I do not see but I am hoping for. My head is covered and protected with salvation. I carry your sword which is Jesus that has manifested into flesh from your Word. Thank you Holy Spirit for dwelling on the inside of me and I repent now for grieving you by the way I live. Lead me in all truth and help me walk this walk out. I can not do it alone but I am leaning and trusting on you. Father I know you hear my prayers and I am confident that you will answer. Thank you Jesus now for blood on the cross that saved all humanity. Receive me into your kingdom to be a servant of you now. Refill and fill me with your Holy Spirit. I will always pray and make supplication to you in the Spirit. I pray Zechariah 9: 12 over my life now. I have come back to the place of safety in you. As a prisoner of Christ, I still have hope in you. You have promised that you will repay me two blessings for each of my troubles. I believe it and I receive it now in Jesus Name. I love you for who you are and all that you have and will do. You are the same in my past, in my present, and my future according to

Hebrews 13: 8. Father God, give me an unexpected encounter with you today so I will never be able to deny you in my flesh again. Regulate my mind now to hear from you. I need you Lord. I have to go in your strength because I can not do it on my own. Carry me when I am weak. Pull me when I don't move, and push me when I am too afraid. I know you are with me always. I love you Lord. I honor you Lord and it is in Jesus Name I pray.

Amen

Combat Declarations and Affirmations

I will not be fearful because you have not given me the spirit of fear, but of power, love and a sound mind. I shall operate in the soundness of my mind. **(Isaiah 41: 10-13, The Message)**

Everyone who has it in for me will end up in the cold. They will become real losers. Those who worked against me and are currently working against me will end up empty-handed with nothing to show for their lives. **(2 Timothy 1:7 KJV)**

I am godly and that is why God has set me apart. The Lord hears my supplications and receives my prayers. He answers me when I call on Him. **(Psalm 4:3, Psalm 6:9)**

I am not fearful, apprehensive, or disappointed. God strengthens and helps me. Everyone who has rose up against me has been put to shame, perplexed and bewildered. Those that are still seeking after me shall not find me. I am hidden and helped in God. **(Isaiah 41: 10-13)**

The Lord helps me and comforts me. He sends me signs of favor and those who harm me are put to shame. Lord thank you for strengthening me and I will not be dismayed. **(Psalm 86: 17)**

The Lord teaches my hands to war and my fingers to fight. **(Psalm 18: 34)**

I am the apple of God's eye and He hides me under the shadow of His wings. I thank you Father because it is you who carries me in your arms and daily loads me with benefits. **(Psalm 17: 8, Psalm 68:19)**

I endure hardship like a good soldier of Jesus Christ. I do not entangle myself with the affairs of this world but I am focused on the spiritual war that I am fighting. **(2 Timothy 2: 3-4)**

My soul is escaped from the snare of the bird. It is broken and my help is in the mere name of the Lord. **(Psalm 124:7)**

The Lord has given me a voice and I am strong. I execute His word and I will endure the day of the Lord because I am safe in Him. **(Joel 2:11)**

Cup of Wine Prayer

"Rather, that the things which the Gentiles sacrifice they sacrifice to demons and not to God, and I do not want you to have fellowship with demons. You cannot drink the cup of the Lord and the cup of demons; you cannot partake of the Lord's table and of the table of demons. Or do we provoke the Lord to jealousy? Are we stronger than He?" **(Psalm 75: 8 NKJV)**

"For the Lord holds a cup in his hand that is full of foaming wine mixed with spices. He pours out the wine in judgment, and all the wicked must drink it, draining it to the dregs." **(Psalms 75:8 NLT)**

Father in the name of Jesus, every cup that has been served to me that I willingly drank or ignorantly drank, I vomit, heave, gag, upchuck, lose, throw up, and regurgitate now in Jesus Name. May the fire of the Holy Ghost clean and purge the residue, the stench, and the contents of what came out through my mouth from my stomach in Jesus Name. May my eyes be open. May my ears be opened. May my heart be receptive to your voice so I will be never partake at the table of demons again. Father forgive me for ever provoking you to jealousy; for you are my Father and I desire to be in right standing with you by the way I live my life. Lord may I eat your daily bread in small increments so I am sure to digest it all. Your bread does not contain any harmful chemicals and it is just right for my spiritual diet. Father I will drink from your fountain so I will never thirst again. I will not be spiritual dehydrated anymore. I will rest in you so I can operate at maximum strength. Every area of my life is ready to be purged by you. May there be a divine exchange right now in Jesus name. Everything that belonged to demons and I drunk it, be choked out by the foaming wine mixed with spices that the Lord holds according to Psalm 75:8. Spiritual and natural regurgitation come upon me now to purify, wash, absolve, and purge me in Jesus. Purify me from my sins and I will be clean. Wash me and I will be whiter than snow. Create in me a clean heart and renew a loyal, steadfast, and pure spirit within me. Restore to me the joy of my salvation and make me willing to obey you. Unseal my lips so the mouth that now praises you if not full of vile, filth, poisonous words, and contamination. But the words I speak are full of abundance in Jesus Name.

Amen

Sinful Nature Prayer

"So now there is no condemnation for those who belong to Christ Jesus. And because you belong to him, the power of the life-giving Spirit has freed you from the power of sin that leads to death. The law of Moses was unable to save us because of the weakness of our sinful nature. So God did what the law could not do. He sent his own Son in a body like the bodies we sinners have. And in that body God declared an end to sin's control over us by giving his Son as a sacrifice for our sins. He did this so that the just requirement of the law would be fully satisfied for us, who no longer follow our sinful nature but instead follow the Spirit. Those who are dominated by the sinful nature think about sinful things, but those who are controlled by the Holy Spirit think about things that please the Spirit. So letting your sinful nature control your mind leads to death. But letting the Spirit control your mind leads to life and peace. For the sinful nature is always hostile to God. It never did obey God's laws, and it never will. That's why those who are still under the control of their sinful nature can never please God." **(Romans 8:1-8 NLT)**

Have mercy upon me, O God, According to Your lovingkindness; According to the multitude of Your tender mercies, Blot out my transgressions. Wash me thoroughly from my iniquity, and cleanse me from my sin. For I acknowledge my transgressions, and my sin *is* always before me. Against You, You only, have I sinned, and done *this* evil in Your sight—That You may be found just when You speak, *and* blameless when You judge. Behold, I was brought forth in iniquity, and in sin my mother conceived me. Behold, You desire truth in the inward parts, and in the hidden *part* You will make me to know wisdom. Purge me with hyssop, and I shall be clean; Wash me, and I shall be whiter than snow. Make me hear joy and gladness, *that* the bones You have broken may rejoice. Hide Your face from my sins, and blot out all my iniquities. Create in me a clean heart, O God, and renew a steadfast spirit within me. Do not cast me away from Your presence, And do not take Your Holy Spirit from me. Restore to me the joy of Your salvation, and uphold me *by Your* generous Spirit. *Then* I will teach transgressors Your ways, and sinners shall be converted to You. **(Psalm 51:1-13)**

Purify me from my sins and I will be clean. Wash me and I will be whiter than snow. Create in me a clean heart and renew a loyal, steadfast, and pure spirit within me. Restore to me the joy of my salvation and make me willing to obey you. Father forgive me for allowing myself to be under the control of my sinful nature. Father help me forgive those who violated me and forced meto be under the control of my sinful nature without my consent or desire. Sanctify me in your truth. Sanctify me in your Word. Teach me to obey your words. Give me grace to obey your Word. Give me the ear of the learned to hear your instructions for my life. Lord help me not reject your counsel and your correction. You disciple me because you love me. I submit wholeheartedly to your rebuke. Fill my mouth with your words because I have hidden your word in my heart. I refuse to willfully and knowingly sin against you. I reject being under the control of my flesh. Help me Lord to crucify my flesh. I nail my flesh and my evil desires to the cross of Christ. Help me to walk upright before you and love your decrees. I declare in my heart that I love your decrees. I will speak your decrees until I see them manifest in my life. I will speak them until they are embedded in my heart. Father, if it is going to happen for my life, it will be by your doing. May your spirit consume me now and show me your way for my life. Lord kill everything in me that has turned against you and everything that was never aligned with who You are and what Your Word declares. Kill it in me Lord. Let me live please but kill it. Lord I stand on Psalm 78:31 today, kill the strongest of my enemies today in Jesus Name.

Amen

Torrential Rain of Fire Prayer

Behold, to morrow about this time I will cause it to rain a very grievous hail, such as hath not been in Egypt since the foundation thereof even until now. **(Exodus 9:18)**

I will summon the sword against you on all the hills of Israel, says the Sovereign Lord. Your men will turn their swords against each other. I will punish you and your armies with disease and bloodshed; I will send torrential rain, hailstones, fire, and burning sulfur! In this way, I will show my greatness and holiness, and I will make myself known to all the nations of the world. Then they will know that I am the Lord. **(Ezekiel 38:12-23)**

But they rebelled, and vexed his Holy Spirit: therefore he was turned to be their enemy, and he fought against them. **(Isaiah 63:10)**

And there fell upon men a great hail out of heaven, every stone about the weight of a talent: and men blasphemed God because of the plague of the hail; for the plague thereof was exceeding great. **(Revelation 16:21)**

Father look down from heaven, behind from your habitation of holiness and glory, where your zeal and strength comes from and hear my prayer. Your name is from everlasting to everlasting. I am asking that you fight on my behalf against every enemy that is indeed your enemy and is trying to destroy my name and destroy my destiny. Father, trample them in your anger. Crush them under your foot in your rage. Fight against them. Bring out your sword and cut them into pieces. May their blood be splattered in the streets for all to see. May their faces be crushed to the ground unrecognizable. Father let my enemies turn their own swords on one another and take each other out. Punish them with disease and famine. Send hailstones, torrential rain, and fire to extinguish and douse the remaining life out of them. May they burn with sulfur in Jesus Name. Father because of the blasphemy that spews from their hearts, may the great hail from heaven fall on them. May the stones that weigh a talent, crush them now in Jesus Name. Father shake the very foundation where they are standing and cause it rain very dreadful hailstones. May those same stones fall on the heads of all those allied with them. Send your thunder, hail, and fire upon the ground that they stand on, to consume their properties and the possessions now in Jesus Name.

Amen

Release From Demonic Dreams Prayer

"But suddenly, your ruthless enemies will be crushed like the finest of dust. Your many attackers will be driven away like chaff before the wind. Suddenly, in an instant, I, the LORD of Heaven's Armies, will act for you with thunder and earthquake and great noise, with whirlwind and storm and consuming fire. All the nations fighting against Jerusalem will vanish like a dream! Those who are attacking her walls will vanish like a vision in the night. A hungry person dreams of eating but wakes up still hungry. A thirsty person dreams of drinking but is still faint from thirst when morning comes. So it will be with your enemies, with those who attack Mount Zion." **(Isaiah 29: 5-8)**

Terror and traps and snares will be your lot, you people of the earth. Those who flee in terror will fall into a trap, and those who escape the trap will be caught in a snare. Destruction falls like rain from the heavens; the foundations of the earth shake. **(Isaiah 24: 17-18)**

At the usual time for offering the evening sacrifice, Elijah the prophet walked up to the altar and prayed, "O Lord, God of Abraham, Isaac, and Jacob, prove today that you are God in Israel and that I am your servant. Prove that I have done all this at your command. O Lord, answer me! Answer me so these people will know that you, O Lord, are God and that you have brought them back to yourself." Immediately the fire of the Lord flashed down from heaven and burned up the young bull, the wood, the stones, and the dust. It even licked up all the water in the trench! And when all the people saw it, they fell face down on the ground and cried out, "The Lord—he is God! Yes, the Lord is God!" (**1 Kings 18: 36- 39**)

When I look at the night sky and see the work of your fingers—the moon and the stars you set in place—what are mere mortals that you should think about them, human beings that you should care for them? (**Psalms 8: 3-4**)

My eyes have seen the downfall of my enemies; my ears have heard the defeat of my wicked opponents. (**Psalms 92: 11**)

Whoever or whatever it is; witch, warlock, wizard, soothsayer, psychic, evil one, occultic, diabolical, cultigents, watcher, or any other demonic entity that fell with satan from Heaven, Father God who sits high and looks low, the Highest God, The One and Only True and Living God, locate these evil beings right now in the mighty name of Jesus. Locate them now Father in the name of the Most High God and destroy them. Jesus paid it all. His job was to come and destroy the works of the enemy. I command the power of God to locate my enemies, to arrest my enemies, destroy them by fire, and destroy all of their plans against me in my dreams. I send the power of Jesus Christ with buckets of blood, swords, javelins, spears, and bombs to blow up the very plans these demonic forces have for my life right now. Jesus destroy their works now. Let the traps, snares, and terror that has been devised for me be my enemies lot today according to Isaiah 24: 17- 18. The Holy One of Israel let every evil dream against my life and destiny catch fire and be consumed right now. Whoever is responsible for this evil dream may the Holy Ghost's Fire chase them down now. By the creative power of the HOLY Spirit inside of me, I reverse every evil effect of Satanic dreams, right now in Jesus Name. Pin them to the ground and suffocate the life out of them with the burning sulfur you have reserved for the final judgment. Even in the days of Elijah the prophet in 1 Kings 18: 36-39 when you sent fire flashing down to consume up the sacrifice, Lord God Almighty, Lord of Heaven's Armies, send that same fire to consume the one responsible for my evil dreams. Destroy them now and all of their evil intentions against me. I command the fire of God to destroy them and Father God sweep their ashes into the Dead Sea in Jesus Name. Suddenly drive them away like chaff before the wind and a send a whirlwind and storm as you did in Isaiah 29: 5-8. Make them vanish like a vision in the night. In the name of Jesus, in the Mighty Name of Jesus, by the precious power and blood of Jesus Christ, destroy them and may they never be my enemy again. No weapon formed against me in my dreams will ever prosper. I burn up every evil dream by the power of the Holy Ghost. Send every conspiracy back to the conspirator. Turn every wicked and perverse act back upon the perverse and wicked one. Make them regret ever plotting against me. Make this disaster that shall come upon them scare other evil beings and keep them from ever planning anything against me. As you created the moons and the stars by your finger and set them in place, take that same finger and castrate, kill and obliterate every enemy that is trying to destroy my name, my destiny, my life, and my health right now in the name of Jesus.

I release myself from the plans and plots of the enemy working against my life. I loose my destiny to move forward in Jesus Name. No weapon formed against me in my dreams will ever prosper. I pray to you Abba Father to give me what is due to me.

Manifest every blessing that has been held up or stopped in Jesus Name. Every good and perfect gift comes from above. Release what is perfect and good to me now in Jesus Name. Lord in Psalms 144: 1 you said that you train my hands for war and give my fingers skill for battle. I am armed for this battle. I have on the belt of truth and the body armour of your righteousness. I have on the shoes of peace. I have the shield of faith held against my heart to stop the fiery arrows of the devil. I have on my helmet of salvation and I am using my sword which is your Word to kill these enemies. Lord send Michael the archangel to fight with any dark kingdom prince, any principality, or any territorial demon that is holding up my answer to this prayers and all other prayers I have sent up to you. Release my angel to deliver the answer now.

Release me from the fiery darts and arrows of the enemy, every demonic device, every demonic distraction and every demonic set back. Father reveal to me every where I have opened a door so I can slam it shut to never open it again. Father forgive me for sinning and willfully sinning against you in times past and even present day. I love you with an everlasting love. I am a doer and not just a hearer of your word. I am not coming with a burnt offering tonight but with a broken and contrite heart that you will not despise. Continue to order my steps and lead me in the paths of righteousness. Even on my most righteous days, I am nothing but a filthy rag. But I present my cleanest, holiest filthy rag to you that I know how. I am coming to you humble yet bold to put a demand on your glory and power today. Just as the young boy in John 9 was born blind so your power could be shown in this earth, let it be so today in my life. I need you to show and up and move now. Only you can destroy my enemies. Only you can send destruction back to the destroyer. Only you can send violence back on the violent one. Only you can send sickness and disease back upon the cursed one. Only you God can do this and deliver. Satan the Lord rebukes you and since His Word and Him are one, He has just spoken. Psalms 92:11 declares "My eyes have seen the downfall of my enemies; my ears have heard the defeat of my wicked opponents". It is finish. It is finish. It is finish. It is finish. It is finish. Satan the Lord has rebuked you and shut up your way. I will lay down in peace and sleep in Jesus Name I pray and seal this prayer with His anointing. 1 John 3: 8 declare the purpose of the Son of God was manifested to destroy the works of the devil. Lord Jesus, Commander and Lord, God over the Heavenly armies fulfill your ministry and neutralize my enemies in your Most High Name I pray.

Amen

Healing Prayer

For I will restore health to you and heal you of your wounds,' says the LORD, 'Because they called you an outcast saying: "This is Zion; No one seeks him." **(Jeremiah 30:17)**

Behold, I will bring your body health and healing; I will heal you and reveal to you the abundance of peace and truth. **(Jeremiah 33:6)**

Now it happened on a certain day, as He was teaching, that there were Pharisees and teachers of the law sitting by, who had come out of every town of Galilee, Judea, and Jerusalem. And the power of the Lord was present to heal them and that same power is to heal you. **(Luke 5: 17)**

Come, and let us return to the LORD; For He has torn, but He will heal us; He has stricken, but He will bind us up. **(Hosea 6:1)**

Bless the LORD, O my soul; And all that is within me, bless His holy name! Bless the LORD, O my soul, And forget not all His benefits: Who forgives all my iniquities, Who heals all of my diseases, Who redeems your life from destruction, Who crowns you with lovingkindness and tender mercies. **(Psalms 103:1-4)**

He sent His word and healed, And delivered him from his destructions. **(Psalms 107:20)**

He heals your broken heart and binds up everyone of your wounds. **(Psalms 147:3)**

O LORD my God, has cried out to You, And You healed him. Manifest your healing. **(Psalms 30:2)**

Is anyone among you sick? Let him call for the elders of the church, and let them pray over him, anointing him with oil in the name of the Lord. And the prayer of faith will save the sick, and the Lord will raise him up. And if he has committed sins, he will be forgiven. Confess your trespasses to one another, and pray for one another, that you may be healed. The effective, fervent prayer of a righteous man avails much. **(James 5:14-16)**

And He said to you, be of good cheer; your faith has made you well. Go in peace. **(Luke 8:48**)

The thief does not come except to steal, and to kill, and to destroy. I have come that they may have life, and that they may have *it* more abundantly. **(John 10:10)**

Behold what manner of love the Father has bestowed on us, that we should be called children of God! Therefore the world does not know us, because it did not know Him. Beloved, now we are children of God; and it has not yet been revealed what we shall be, but we know that when He is revealed, we shall be like Him, for we shall see Him as He is. And everyone who has this hope in Him purifies himself, just as He is pure. **(1 John 3: 1-2)**

Father in the name of Jesus Christ of Nazareth, I am calling on the one whose chief objective for sending Jesus into this world was to heal the sick and save the lost. Allow me to find and declare your word so it can heal me. It was sent out to heal me and I receive my healing in all areas of my life now in Jesus Name. Recondition and fine- tune my health now. Heal every wound that I have and heal every place that I am hurting. Bring healing to my mind and body. Reveal to me and give me an abundance of peace and truth. Your word is truth and I receive it now in Jesus Name. As you heal me, you are releasing, liberating, emancipating, and delivering me from devastation and crowning me with tender mercies. Father I acknowledge, salute you, and I receive my healing now in Jesus Name.

Amen

Rivers of Blood Prayer

"For he turned their rivers into blood, so no one could drink from the streams. He sent vast swarms of flies to consume them and hordes of frogs to ruin them. He gave their crops to caterpillars; their harvest was consumed by locusts. He destroyed their grapevines with hail and shattered their sycamore-figs with sleet. He abandoned their cattle to the hail, their livestock to bolts of lightning." **(Psalms 78:44-48 NLT)**

Father in the name of Jesus Christ, every wicked and evil person that is attacking me and trying to offset my course in you, I stand on Psalm 78: 44-48. Turn their rivers into blood. Abba send vast swarms of flies and frogs to consume them. Father give their crops to caterpillars and their harvest to locust. May they not reap the benefits of their labor and may they not proposer off of what is good. Father destroy their grapevines with hail and shatter their sycamore figs with sleet. Send a torrential rainstorm from heaven to utterly destroy all of their harvest. Allow their cattle and livestock to be abandoned to the hail to be beaten, bruised, and out to death. Allow bolts of lightning to scare and destroy their cattle in Jesus Name.

Amen

Wind of God Prayer

Then Moses stretched out his hand over the sea; and the LORD swept the sea back by a strong east wind all night and turned the sea into dry land, so the waters were divided. The sons of Israel went through the midst of the sea on the dry land, and the waters were like a wall to them on their right hand and on their left. **(Exodus 14:21-22)**

The LORD shifted the wind to a very strong west wind which took up the locusts and drove them into the Red Sea; not one locust was left in all the territory of Egypt". **(Exodus 10: 19)**

And suddenly there came from heaven a noise like a violent rushing wind, and it filled the whole house where they were sitting". Father speak like thunder and when you come Holy Spirit, do not be silent. Fill our houses, our temples with your glory and with your presence. **(Acts 2: 2)**

"For behold, He who forms mountains and creates the wind And declares to man what are His thoughts, He who makes dawn into darkness And treads on the high places of the earth, The LORD God of hosts is His name". **(Amos 4: 13)**

Therefore, thus says the Lord GOD, "I will make a violent wind break out in My wrath. There will also be in My anger a flooding rain and hailstones to consume it in wrath. **(Ezekiel 13:13)**

When the south wind blew softly, supposing that they had obtained their desire, putting out to sea, they sailed close by Crete. But not long after, a tempestuous head wind arose, called Euroclydon. **(Acts 27: 13-14)**

"He caused the east wind to blow in the heavens And by His power He directed the south wind". **(Psalm 78: 26)**

The hand of the Lord came upon me and brought me out in the Spirit of the Lord, and set me down in the midst of the valley; and it *was* full of bones. Then He caused me to pass by them all around, and behold, *there were* very many in the open valley; and indeed *they were* very dry. And He said to me, "Son of man, can these bones live?" So I answered, "O Lord God, You know." Again He said to me, "Prophesy to these bones, and say to them, 'O dry bones, hear the word of the Lord! **5** Thus says the Lord God to these bones: "Surely I will cause breath to enter into you, and you shall live. I will put sinews on you and bring flesh upon you, cover you with skin and put breath in you; and you shall live. Then you shall know that I *am* the Lord." So I prophesied as I was commanded; and as I prophesied, there was a noise, and suddenly a rattling; and the bones came together, bone to bone. Indeed, as I looked, the sinews and the flesh came upon them, and the skin covered them over; but *there was* no breath in them. Also He said to me, "Prophesy to the breath, prophesy, son of man, and say to the breath, 'Thus says the Lord God: "Come from the four winds, O breath, and breathe on these slain, that they may live." So I prophesied as He commanded me, and breath came into them, and they lived, and stood upon their feet, an exceedingly great army. Then He said to me, "Son of man, these bones are the whole house of Israel. They indeed say, 'Our bones are dry, our hope is lost, and we ourselves are cut off!' Therefore prophesy and say to them, 'Thus says the Lord God: "Behold, O My people, I will open your graves and cause you to come up from your graves, and bring you into the land of Israel.

Then you shall know that I *am* the Lord, when I have opened your graves, O My people, and brought you up from your graves. I will put My Spirit in you, and you shall live, and I will place you in your own land. Then you shall know that I, the Lord, have spoken *it* and performed *it*," says the Lord.' **(Ezekiel 37: 1-14)**

Father release the east winds in the heavens to blow every blessing and promise that you have for my life today in Jesus Name. Give me this day my daily bread. Give me enough bread for today. Father thank you. Father I love you. Father I honor you. Father guide the south wind by your mighty power to blow away every enemy in my life. Father let the south wind blow out of me every wicked and perverse thought. Father let the south blow away every hidden agenda, jealous and envious way, and every ungodly action. Father help me be more like you and nothing like my flesh. Father guide the south wind with your mighty power and release a wind in my life that will revive me to a new level in you. Revive me to a new place in you. Revive me and propel me further in you. Wind of God blow your strength in me. Blow your grace on me. Blow your love in me. Blow your peace and joy on me. Blow long-suffering and hope in you on me. Father I thank you. Father I love you. Father I honor you. Father I love you. Father I worship you. Father I adore you and miss you. I want to spend more time with you. Father may you send a strong east wind to part every sea of affliction, sea of strife, sea of bitterness, sea of anger, sea of distraction, and sea of division away from me now in Jesus Name. Father may you send a strong west wind to blow away every enemy of my destiny, every enemy of my family, every enemy of my life, and every enemy on the inside of me. Lord send a strong west wind to blow it out of my life and away from me forever in Jesus Name. Lord God of Host turn the light of counterfeit angels into darkness now. Every angel of light that has not been sent by you, turn off their lights now in Jesus Name. Send the fire of the Holy Ghost to burn up their light. May the flame of fire on the inside of me put off the dim, dull, and demonic lights of our enemies in Jesus Name. Father make violent wind break out over every enemy in my life. Lord may your wrath break out of secret enemies, enemies yet to be exposed, enemies that pose as friend but are really foes. Lord send your violent wind to break up their plans, plots, and ploys in Jesus Name. Father, due to your righteous anger, send flooding rains and hailstones to consume them now in Jesus Name. May sudden destruction come upon them unaware.

Father send your Euroclydon, Your East wind to blow away everything that is vexing you in my life. For every sin and every iniquity in my life, send the Euroclydon wind to destroy it now in Jesus Name. Every idol, every weight, every excuse, and every unrighteous idea, thought, and imagination, I cast them down and ask that your Euroclydon wind comes to destroy them in Jesus Name. Your force is so mighty and your majesty is so glorious. Father I need the wind of God to blow until it has put out every strange fire that is burning in and around my life through association, violations, or isolation, may the fire of the living God and your wind to cause this to happen now in Jesus Name. Father may the North wind that is blowing in heaven to blow every blessing and every promise that you have for my life. May your power direct the south wind in the direction my blessing and promise should blow. I catch it by the breathe and hands of God in Jesus Name. Father release the North winds in the heavens to blow every blessing and promise that you have for my life today in Jesus Name. Give me this day my daily bread. Give me enough bread for today. Father thank you. Father I love you. Father I honor you. Father guide the south wind by your mighty power to blow away every enemy in my life. Father let the south wind blow out of me every wicked and perverse thought. Father let the south guide blow away every hidden agendas, jealous and envious way, and ungodly action. Father help me be more like you and none of my fleshly self. Father guide the south wind with your mighty power and release a wind in my life that will revive me to a new level in you, that will revive me to a new place in you, that will revive me and propel me further in you. Wind of God blow your strength in me. Blow your grace on me. Blow your love in me. Blow your peace and joy on me. Blow long-suffering and hope in you on me. Father I thank you. Father I love you. Father I honor you. Father I love you. Father I worship you. Father I adore you and miss you. I want to spend more time with you. Please forgive me for not making you priority since being home but I want to spend intimate time with you, enjoying who you are, communing with you, and giving you my undivided attention.

Amen

The Breaker's Prayer

"God is honored in Judah; his name is great in Israel. Jerusalem is where he lives; Mount Zion is his home. There he has broken the fiery arrows of the enemy, the shields and swords and weapons of war. Interlude" **(Psalms 76:1-3 NLT)**

Let the sinners be consumed out of the earth, and let the wicked be no more. Bless thou the Lord, O my soul. Praise ye the Lord. **(Psalm 104: 35)**

I will surely assemble, O Jacob, all of thee; I will surely gather the remnant of Israel; I will put them together as the sheep of Bozrah, as the flock in the midst of their fold: they shall make great noise by reason of the multitude of men. The breaker is come up before them: they have broken up, and have passed through the gate, and are gone out by it: and their king shall pass before them, and the Lord on the head of them. **(Micah 2: 12- 13)**

The Lord of hosts has sworn, saying, "Surely, as I have thought, so it shall come to pass, And as I have purposed, *so* it shall stand: That I will break the Assyrian in My land,

And on My mountains tread him underfoot. Then his yoke shall be removed from them, And his burden removed from their shoulders. **(Isaiah 14: 24-25)**

Then I returned and considered all the oppression that is done under the sun: And look! The tears of the oppressed, But they have no comforter— On the side of their oppressors *there is* power, But they have no comforter. **(Ecclesiastes 4: 1)**

"For God says, "I will break the strength of the wicked, but I will increase the power of the godly." **(Psalm 75:10 NLT)**

God is a just judge, And God is angry with the wicked every day. **(Psalm 7:11)**

Behold, I give unto you power to tread on serpents and scorpions, and over all the power of the enemy: and nothing shall by any means hurt you. Notwithstanding in this rejoice not, that the spirits are subject unto you; but rather rejoice, because your names are written in heaven. **(Luke 10: 19-20)**

"You shall not permit a sorceress to live. **(Exodus 22: 18)**

Behold, *the wicked* brings forth iniquity; Yes, he conceives trouble and brings forth falsehood. He made a pit and dug it out, And has fallen into the ditch *which* he made. His trouble shall return upon his own head, And his violent dealing shall come down on his own crown. **(Psalm 7: 14-16)**

He loosed on them his fierce anger— all his fury, rage, and hostility. He dispatched against them a band of destroying angels." **(Psalms 78:49 NLT)**

Abba Father, may I be the sacrifice today so the same fire that fell from Mt. Carmel, can fall on and in me. I want that same fire so when I get ready to step into a hellish situation you can bring me out without getting burned or smelling like smoke. Father break the fiery arrows of mine enemies. Father break the shields, swords, and weapons of war of my enemies in Jesus Name. Father loose your fierce anger on my enemies. Father release all your fury, release all your rage, release all of your hostility on my enemies. Dispatch your destroying angels to utterly destroy every enemy in my life. Destroy the enemies I know about, the secrets ones, the hidden ones, the ones lying dormant, and the ones on the way. Lord dispatch your destroying angels now to fulfill their assignment to utterly destroy them. Let my enemies be consumed out of the earth now. Let the wicked be ruined beyond recovery. Father you are the breaker and I am calling forth your breaking power to break my enemies into bits of smithereens. May their remains be as shard. Son of Man, break their bows and make the war against my life cease. Cut their spears in half. Burn their modes of transportation with Holy Ghost fire. Father break the strength of these wicked doers and increase my power now in Jesus Name. You have given me power to trample and plod on serpents and scorpions. I now use my power to plod and trample upon every scorpion and serpent in my life. Thank you Abba that nothing else will by any means hurt me. These evil spirits will not hurt me. I stand in triumph now to know that my name is written in the lamb's book of life. It is an honor and privilege to serve you.

Father according to Jeremiah 50, May my enemies be shamed, their idols humiliated, and their images broken into pieces. Nations will rise against them and there will be continual weeping among them. I shall plunder my enemies and be satisfied. Since you have contended against the Lord, He has bought out His weapons of indignation against you and you will be made heaps of ruin. Your young shall fall in the streets and your men of war shall be cut off. A drought will be found upon you, as the sword of the Lord will be against your treasures. Your entire army will be destroyed for the Lord will swallow you up like a monster and crush you.

Break every satanic conspiracy over my life. I command the source of my enemies to dry up completely in Jesus Name. No regroups, no refuel, and no gatherings against me in Jesus Name. I command the earth to reject and swallow my enemies up in Jesus Name. Lord send your clean up crew to gather the waste of my enemies and throw their remains in Sheol in Jesus Name.

Amen

Dispatchers Prayer

And Jesus went about all the cities and villages, teaching in their synagogues, and preaching the gospel of the kingdom, and healing every sickness and every disease among the people. But when he saw the multitudes, he was moved with compassion on them, because they fainted, and were scattered abroad, as sheep having no shepherd. Then saith he unto his disciples, The harvest truly is plenteous, but the labourers are few; Pray ye therefore the Lord of the harvest, that he will send forth labourers into his harvest. **(Matthew 9; 35- 38)**

May I be discharged and dispatched today into the vineyard of soul winning. Father you have commissioned me to become part of the ministry of reconciliation. Anoint me and prepare me to be your laborer going to gather the end-time harvest. Father in the name of Jesus, increase the employment rate of Heaven today. May I be a good steward over the souls you have given me access to. There are souls in the grocery store that I see and can witness to. May you give me the boldness and courage to witness to them when I see them there. There are souls in the mall when I go shopping. Give me the boldness and courage to witness to them. There are souls at school when I am at one. Give me the boldness and courage to witness there. There are souls in the gym, at the movies, and in the bowling alleys. Give me the boldness and courage to witness to them. There are souls when I am in a restaurant, and even in the church. May you give me a courageous boldness to witness to them. There are souls on my job and in my business. There are souls that need to be saved in my family. May you give me the boldness and courage to do so.

Father help me be a good steward over the souls I have access to. Lord lead me to the harvest field. Open my eyes to see and anoint me to win souls for You, in Jesus Name.

Amen

Fallen Enemy Prayer

"And he said unto them, I beheld Satan as lightning fall from heaven. Behold, I give unto you power to tread on serpents and scorpions, and over all the power of the enemy: and nothing shall by any means hurt you. Notwithstanding in this rejoice not, that the spirits are subject unto you; but rather rejoice, because your names are written in heaven.' **(Luke 10:18-20 KJV)**

Joshua therefore came upon them suddenly, having marched all night from Gilgal. So the Lord routed them before Israel, killed them with a great slaughter at Gibeon, chased them along the road that goes to Beth Horon, and struck them down as far as Azekah and Makkedah. And it happened, as they fled before Israel *and* were on the descent of Beth Horon, that the Lord cast down large hailstones from heaven on them as far as Azekah, and they died. *There were* more who died from the hailstones than the children of Israel killed with the sword. **(Joshua 10: 9-11)**

But You, O Lord, shall laugh at them; You shall have all the nations in derision. I will wait for You, O You his Strength; For God *is* my defense. My God of mercy shall come to meet me; God shall let me see *my desire* on my enemies. Do not slay them, lest my people forget; Scatter them by Your power, And bring them down, O Lord our shield. *For* the sin of their mouth *and* the words of their lips, Let them even be taken in their pride, And for the cursing and lying *which* they speak. Consume *them* in wrath, consume *them*, That they *may* not *be;* And let them know that God rules in Jacob To the ends of the earth. *Selah*.. **(Psalm 59: 8-13)**

Everything that satan has stolen from you has just fallen from the sky and you shall recover your plunder, your ready plunder tonight in Jesus Name. Father as you have declared that no scorpion, no serpent, and no snake, shall harm or crush us, we speak with Holy Ghost boldness and authority, that no scorpion, no serpent, and no snake, shall harm or crush us. Thank you Father that none of these evils will put a hand on us, put a hand on our children, put a hand on our children's children or even a generation not yet born. Father thank you for the triumph over these evils and over the authority you have given us that these evils obey us, but more importantly because our names are written in the lambs book of life. May the cement of the third heaven be thrown down and fall threw the second heaven destroying and plundering every enemy satan has planted and stationed in and around my life in Jesus Name. May my goods fall to the ground as I am ready to recover my prepared loot. Father may the sword that satan has in his lips be used to cut out his own tongue. Laugh at him and seen him in derision and disparagement. Mock him. God you are my defense. So I ask you to devour satan in your wrath.

Amen

satan Clause Prayer

And no marvel; for satan himself is transformed into an angel of light. **(2 Corinthians 11:14)**

I heard God say to me on August 4, 2017 around 10:00 pm after I came in from a prayer meeting satan clause, satan claus.. Like santa claus... I was thinking what does this mean? My spiritual mother taught me that santa is satan scrambled. Do not be deceived and do not let your children be deceived at the angel of light of santa. God said to me satan claus. A clause can be considered a legal written document and it can also mean by way of intimidation. The enemy has some written documents and decrees against us that must be burned with the fire of the Holy Ghost. Some are based on facts and some have been fabricated, but God is prepared to dismiss the case against you and declare your innocence and proclaim your not guilty verdict. In addition, the enemy has made some of us think that if we contest for what he has stolen from us, that we will lose all that we have now. But the Lord is ready to expose the enemy and declare that as you war in prayer and with his Word, you shall win and win well in Jesus Name.

Father in the name of Jesus Christ, every contract and written order that has been transcribed and scripted about me, I call forth fire from heaven where you reside to destroy it now. Expunge every record that has been written about me, true or false. You have forgiven me of my sins so Abba wash away every ungodly word composed about me. Everywhere my name is being called, may the blood of Jesus answer for me. As my name is being called for a diabolical purpose, may my enemies choke on the blood of Jesus. May they gag and not be able to speak. I snatch out the voice box of every enemy speaking against my life and those who have written evil decrees about me. I now sign a contract soaked in the blood of Jesus and I put a hit out on every devil and demon that is tracking my steps, monitoring me, and eavesdropping. Father dispatch full-size, colossal, sparring, and militant angels to go to bout and win on my behalf. Thank you for scorching every clause, every contract, and every note that has been passed around about your servant that was created from the pits of hell. Every godly, wholesome, and righteous contract that is rightfully mine, I call it forth now in Jesus Name. Every inheritance that I am due, I summons it to locate me now. I do not belong to the enemy and I sever all ties to Satan in Jesus Name. I renounce any partnerships or deals with Satan. Satan, the Lord rebukes you. I reject your advances and propositions. I am God's servant and I am God's warrior. I am the child of the Most High God. I am seated in Heavenly places in Christ Jesus, far above all principalities and powers of satan; for you are under my feet.

Amen

An APB Prayer

Then God stepped in and spoke to Elijah the Tishbite, "On your feet; go down and confront Ahab of Samaria, king of Israel. You'll find him in the vineyard of Naboth; he's gone there to claim it as his own. Say this to him: 'God's word: What's going on here? First murder, then theft?' Then tell him, 'God's verdict: The very spot where the dogs lapped up Naboth's blood, they'll lap up your blood—that's right, *your* blood." **(1 Kings 21: 19)**

"Let us break their bonds in pieces And cast away their cords from us." He who sits in the heavens shall laugh; The Lord shall hold them in derision. Then He shall speak to them in His wrath, And distress them in His deep displeasure: "Yet I have set My King

On My holy hill of Zion." "I will declare the decree: The Lord has said to Me, 'You *are* My Son, Today I have begotten You. Ask of Me, and I will give *You* The nations *for* Your inheritance, And the ends of the earth *for* Your possession. You shall break them with a rod of iron; You shall dash them to pieces like a potter's vessel." **(Psalm 2: 3-9)**

I cried to the Lord with my voice, And He heard me from His holy hill. *Selah*. I lay down and slept; I awoke, for the Lord sustained me. I will not be afraid of ten thousands of people who have set *themselves* against me all around. Arise, O Lord; Save me, O my God! For You have struck all my enemies on the cheekbone; You have broken the teeth of the ungodly. Salvation *belongs* to the Lord. Your blessing *is* upon your people. **(Psalm 3: 4-8)**

You have rebuked the nations, You have destroyed the wicked; You have blotted out their name forever and ever. O enemy, destructions are finished forever! And you have destroyed cities; Even their memory has perished. But the Lord shall endure forever; He has prepared His throne for judgment. **(Psalm 9: 5-7)**

The nations have sunk down in the pit *which* they made; In the net which they hid, their own foot is caught. The Lord is known *by* the judgment He executes; The wicked is snared in the work of his own hands. *Selah*. The wicked shall be turned into hell, *And* all the nations that forget God. For the needy shall not always be forgotten; The expectation of the poor shall *not* perish forever. Arise, O Lord, Do not let man prevail; Let the nations be judged in Your sight. **(Psalm 9: 15-19)**

May the Lord cut off all flattering lips, *and* the tongue that speaks proud things. **(Psalm 12: 3)**

He teacheth my hands to war, so that a bow of steel is broken by mine arms. **(Psalm 18: 34)**

An all-points bulletin is also known as an APB. In America and Canada, this is a broadcast system used by law enforcement to communicate with those parties who work with and work in conjunction with law enforcement. This bulletin is usually comprised of data about people who have committed a crime or a person who is suspected to have committed a crime. The enemy of my life and the enemy of my destiny is wanted by the Lord of Heaven's Armies. I am sending out a spiritual APB (all points bulletin) for their arrest, trial, and execution now in Jesus Name.

Father you have determined that the path of the wicked leads to destruction. Destruction has come today to the enemy of my destiny today. In the name of Jesus may the blood of Jesus and the light of the Holy Ghost zero in on my enemy right now. Hold your blood soaked spear, javelin, and sword to their necks. Lord laugh at them while you vex them because of your displeasure. I am not asking for my enemy to be my inheritance, but I am asking that you break their necks with a rod of iron and dash them into pieces like a potter's jar. Vengeance belongs to you and today is the day you shall avenge for me. Lord you hate my bloody and deceitful enemies. Destroy them now and let them fall at their own counsel. Because of their wickedness, you have been angry with them everyday. May they fall and perish at your sight. Lord may they be snared by the works of their hands. Father rain snares, fire and brimstone now in Jesus Name. Lord in addition to that, drop hail stones and coals of fire on their heads. Shoot them with lightning in Jesus Name. Cut off their flattering lips and cut out their tongue. Point your arrows at their face and release them now. May dogs come to lick up their blood. Thank you for the great deliverance now in Jesus Name.

Amen

Back Slider Prayer

Father, I am calling for souls today in the kingdom in Jesus Name. According to Psalm 94: 17, "Lord unless you were my help, my soul would have dwelt in silence. But you Lord are my defense. You are the rock of my refuge. Father I call you Mighty King, lover of justice. Your unfailing love endures forever, your faithfulness extends to every generation. Father you sit on your throne forever, your fame endures to every generation. Lord your commands have no limit. You're a limitless God. Father you are the God who listens to the prayers of the destitute and you do not reject their pleas. Heaven is the work of your hand. You are the same and your years have no end. I praise you with my whole heart. Psalms 103: 2- 6 declares, "Bless the Lord, O my soul, And forget not all His benefits: Who forgives all our iniquities, Who heals all our diseases, Who redeems our life from destruction, Who crowns us with loving kindness and tender mercies, Who satisfies our mouth with good things, So that our youth is renewed like the eagle's. The Lord executes righteousness, And justice for all who are oppressed". You are the God who is compassionate and merciful. You're the God who is slow to get angry but full of unfailing love. You are the same God of war and Jesus leads Heaven's Army. You're the God that doesn't even give us what we deserve.

Lord, transform my mind into a new person by the way I think. Lord, let me learn your will for my life which is good, pleasing, acceptable, and the perfect will of you. Father I shall sanctify myself with the truth and the truth is your Word according to John 17:17. Jesus transform my mind today. I exchange my carnal thinking and fleshly thinking for the mind of Christ. For I do not have a spirit of fear, but of power, love, and a sound mind. Thank you for a sound mind. Thank you for a peaceful mind. Thank you for a healthy and whole mind. Thank you for a mind that cast down vain imaginations and thinks on things that are good and acceptable Hallelujah in Jesus Name.

Create in me a clean heart and renew a right, loyal, and steadfast spirit in me. Father help me give instructions with kindness in Jesus Name. Father help me bear my own burdens. Help me not think highly of myself. Father let me examine my own work and let me bear my own load.

Father let every backslider that belongs in your house return to you now in Jesus Name. Gather them from every city and send them to the appropriately house in where they will be planted and flourish. Father the two from each family that should return to you, I call their souls back to you now in Jesus Name. I call my family members by name now and say return back to God. Father thank you for the good shepherds who rules your way. Thank you Father for the good shepherd you have given me that rules well. Thank you for the shepherds who will rule well over those who will return back to you.

Add daily to the house of the Lord who are being save. Father give me a spirit of meekness so I can help restore those who backslid, have backslid, or will backslid. Father help me live out Galatians 6:1 that tells me if a brother or sister is overtaken in a fault, if I am spiritual, I should restore them with a spirit of meekness. Father forgive me if I have gossiped about people instead of restoring them. Father forgive me if I have condemned people instead of loving them and giving them your truth. Father forgive me if I gave people bad news instead of the Good News of Jesus Christ. Father forgive me and restore unto me your meekness. Father restore those who need restoring in Jesus Name. Father let the spirit of rejection die in me and those in a backslidden state. Father let me not reject those who once was a brother and sister in my church, in my ministry, and in the body of Christ, but let me love all people. Father help me not make my brothers and sisters feel outcasts but really love on them.

Holy Spirit help me not be legalistic but spirit led. I break off the influence of the world off of my mind now in Jesus Name. Put the cross of Christ between me and anything that is keeping me from being in your will. Father keep me from aligning myself with the world. Set a wall of fire around my emotions today. Harness my emotions in Jesus Name. Father I am asking for divine self control. Set a watch over the door of my lips and let my words be seasoned with salt in Jesus Name. If another believer is overcome by some sin, Father help me to gently and humbly help them back on the right path. As I am helping someone else, Father let me be careful not to fall into the same temptation.

Father I do not want to be a fool, and I do not want to fool ourselves. I reject the praises of every fool that has ever spoken in my life. Jesus help me pay careful attention to my own work, so I will never compare myself to someone else. Father let every divisive, competitive, and comparative spirit die in me in Jesus Name. I take the fire of the Holy Ghost and his blood-soaked grenades and burn up and blow up every divisive spirit that is in operation now. I snuff you out and uproot you now in Jesus Name. Send unity into the camp of your believers. Break into pieces every design of confusion and strife in Jesus Name. I snatch out the voice box of every enemy that is speaking against our houses, against our local churches and assemblies, against the leadership of our churches and assemblies, and the members, current ones and those on the way now in Jesus Name. I shall increase on every side and it shall start from the head and flow down. Father I get under the covering and authority of my pastor in Jesus Name. Father I recommit to being submissive to the shepherd you have placed to guard over my soul. My pastor shall guard over my soul will great joy and not grief in Jesus Name. Forgive me for any secret envy, any secret jealousy, any secret plans, plots, motives, and agendas that would bring strife to my pastor, my leaders, other members, and my church in Jesus Name. Forgive me Jesus. Forgive me for not standing up and defending your appointed vessels. Forgive me Jesus and restore me and divinely realign me with the vision and mission of your church as it is a part of the body of Christ and Kingdom of God.

Father, I know I am responsible for my own conduct. Because I am taught the word of God, give me a heart to provide for your teachers, your leaders, and your pastors, sharing all good things with them and never evil.

Every married couple that I know that has backslid, I call their souls to slide back to you now in Jesus Name. Every set of siblings that I know and you have called, I call their souls back to you now in Jesus Name. Every mother and daughter that has backslid, may they return to you. Every father and son who has backslid, may they return to you in Jesus Name. Every dating couple who has slid back from you, may they return in Jesus Name. Children who have backslid, may they return to you. Every family member, every friend, every brother and sister in Christ that has backslid, may they return to you in Jesus Name. Holy Ghost come and when you come, do not be silent!!! Holy Ghost come and when you come do not come empty handed!!!! Holy Ghost come and bring souls with you.

Father I know that the harvest is plenty but the laborers are few. Father send laborers now in Jesus Name. Create in me a spirit to labor and gather your sheep. Father raise me up to share the good news of Jesus Christ and invite souls into your house. Father give me a burden to win souls and to see lives changed. Thank you Father for snatching me. Thank you Father that although my sin warranted death, you gave me life and life more abundantly. Father fill your sanctuaries with souls. Father point me in the direction of those who are assigned to the seats in your church. Father point me in the right location to witness and share the unadulterated Word of God with people. Open up doors on my job, in my home, in my community, and in my sphere of influence to share the gospel of Jesus Christ. Father gather these souls today from wherever they are scattered and send them in Jesus Name. May I be a good steward of the souls you have given me access to. I thank you for the great increase and harvest of souls that will come into the kingdom. I glorify and honor you in Jesus Name.

Amen.

Benediction

Father I pray Psalms 90: 17 over every reader of this book. May the Lord our God show you his approval and make your efforts successful, Yes, make your efforts successful!

May The Lord bless you. May the Lord keep you. May The Lord make his face shine upon you, and be gracious unto you. May The Lord lift up his countenance upon you, and give you peace. And you shall put His name upon the children of Israel, upon the children you teach, the children you have, and the children you have access to, and God will bless them. I come against backlash, revenge, and retaliation now in Jesus Name. I seal these prayers in the blood of Jesus. For God has done it for you. The Lord God Almighty has went before you and he will satisfy us with good things. I love you today and forever more. Be blessed in Jesus Name.

Your Warrior Sister,

Simene'